# Contents

KU-683-696

Some words are shown in bold, **like this**.
You can find them in the glossary on page 23.

# What is a scorpion?

fat-tailed scorpion

Scorpions are a type of **arachnid**.

Spiders are also types of arachnids.

giant hairy **desert** scorpion

exoskeleton

Like spiders, scorpions have eight legs.

They have a hard body, called an
**exoskeleton**.

# Where do scorpions live?

United States

Middle East

Africa

deserts

The scorpions in this book live in the hot, dry **deserts** of the United States, Africa, and the Middle East.

Can you find these deserts on the map?

burrow

The desert is sandy or rocky.

The scorpions live in **burrows** that they dig in the ground.

# What do scorpions look like?

**Desert** scorpions are brown, black, or yellow.

Most scorpions are smaller than your hand.

At the front of their bodies, scorpions have two **pincers**.

They have a curled-over tail, with a sharp sting at the end.

# What do scorpions do at night?

It is very hot in the **desert** in the day but it gets cooler at night.

This is when desert scorpions come out of their **burrows** to look for food.

hair

A scorpion cannot see very well.

It uses tiny hairs on its body to pick up movements made by its **prey**.

# What do scorpions eat?

lizard

**Desert** scorpions mostly eat **insects**, spiders, and small lizards.

These animals are also out and about at night.

pincer

The scorpion sits and waits for its **prey** to come close.

Then it grabs it in its **pincers** and stings it to stop it moving.

# Do scorpions live alone?

**Desert** scorpions live and hunt alone.

They only meet other scorpions when it is time to **mate**.

The male and female scorpions do a special dance.

They dance around in circles and lift their stingers over their backs.

# What do baby scorpions look like?

baby scorpion

Baby scorpions are born at night.

They look like tiny adults but they cannot sting.

The babies ride on their mother's back for about a week.

Then they are old enough to look after themselves.

# What hunts scorpions?

owl

Animals such as owls, lizards, and bats hunt **desert** scorpions.

Like the scorpions, these animals are active at night.

sting

If there is danger, the scorpion lifts its tail up and stings.

Its sting is **poisonous** and can cause pain or even death.

# What do scorpions do in the day?

In the day, **desert** scorpions hide away in their **burrows**.

It is much cooler underground.

Scorpions do not sleep in the same way that you do, but they rest instead.

In the evening, they set out hunting again.

# Scorpion body map

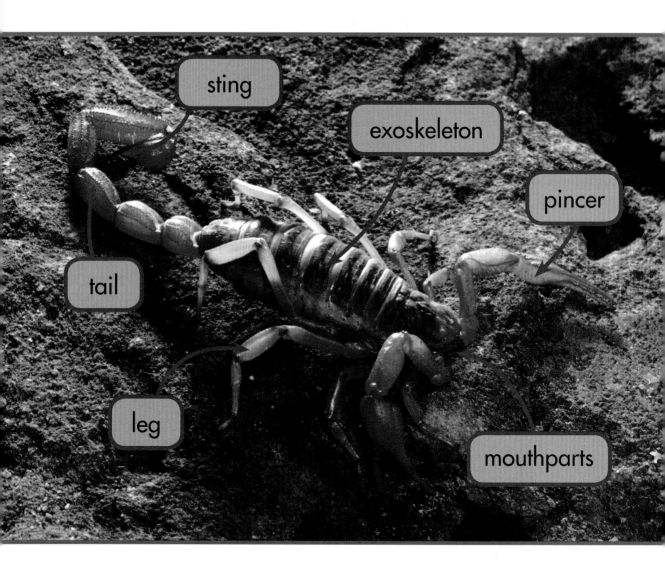

sting

exoskeleton

pincer

tail

leg

mouthparts

# Glossary

 **arachnid** animal with eight legs, such as a spider or scorpion

 **burrow** hole in the ground where an animal lives

 **desert** very dry place that is rocky, stony, or sandy

 **exoskeleton** hard outside of a scorpion's body

 **insect** animal that has six legs, such as a grasshopper

 **mate** when a male and female animal have babies

 **pincer** large claw on a scorpion's body

 **poisonous** may cause illness or death

 **prey** animals that are eaten by other animals

# Find out more

## Books

*Desert Animals* (Focus on Habitats), Stephen Savage (Wayland, 2006)

*Deserts* (My World of Geography), Angela Royston (Heinemann Library, 2004)

*24 Hours: Desert* (Focus on Habitats), Elizabeth Haldane (Dorling Kindersley, 2006)

## Websites

Find out lots of interesting things about scorpions at:
www.sandiegozoo.org/animalbytes/t-scorpion.html

Learn more about the giant desert hairy scorpion at:
www.thebigzoo.com/Animals/Giant_Desert_Hairy_Scorpion.asp

# Index